exciti...
to make w...
wool
string and thread

about this book

This do-it-yourself craft book is specially designed for children. Every page has such clear step-by-step pictures and easy-to-follow words that you can do everything on your own without grown-up help. And once you see how the projects work, you'll be inspired to make dozens of creative things!

This book is about all sorts of beautiful yarns like wool and string and raffia and embroidery cottons. The chapters are arranged in a progression, with the easier projects at the beginning and the more difficult ones at the end. In many cases the methods in one chapter lead to methods in the next chapter so it's a good idea to follow the order of the book.

The pink tags at the side of the page tell you the method the chapter explains – all the projects between one tag and the next are based on the same method.

The 'Try it first' tags at the top of the page indicate practice sections. These help you to understand how a method works with a simple project before starting on something bigger and more exciting. It also means you can experiment with odds and ends rather than using specially-bought wools. Then it does not matter if the first try doesn't work out too well.

Before you start, it's helpful to read through the Useful Things to Know pages overleaf.

Useful things to know

When you start on a project, look through the whole chapter first so you have a picture in your mind of what you are going to do. Then get together all the things you will need.

Try to clear yourself as much space to work in as possible. If the project involves anything messy like glue or paint make sure you cover everything within possible splashing distance—floor, table, walls— with thick newspaper. Cover yourself too with an apron, overall or old shirt. Have an old cloth so you can clean your hands as you go along.

When you've finished, always clear up blobs of paint and glue quickly, otherwise they may not come out. Roll up newspaper carefully, with all the rubbish inside, and throw it away. Take care to put lids back on glue.

Be a collector. Don't throw away any scraps of wool or string left over from a project—keep them in a large envelope. They will come in useful for lots of other projects.

Different kinds of yarn

Knitting wool comes in various thicknesses. If you untwist a piece of knitting wool you will see that it is made of several strands. According to the number of strands it is called 2-ply, 3-ply or 4-ply. Double knitting wool is thicker than 4-ply wool.

Tapestry wool is like knitting wool, but is a bit firmer and tougher. It comes in smaller amounts than knitting wool.

Rug wool is like very thick, tough

Various kinds of board

Cardboard is like a very thick paper. Collect cereal packets and free cartons from the supermarket.

Corrugated cardboard is made of two layers of cardboard stuck together. One layer is ridged.

Softboard (also called insulating board) is soft and light. It is usually about 1·5cm thick.

Plywood is made from very thin layers of wood glued together like a sandwich.

Cork tiles are squares of cork, usually about 30cm square and 3mm thick.

Polystyrene tiles are also usually 30cm square and come in different thicknesses.

You can buy softboard, plywood and the tiles from a handyman's shop.

Other things

Hessian is like sacking, with threads that are easy to count.

Felt is a soft cloth made of matted wool. It can be bought in small squares or by the metre.

Pencils. The most useful sort is called HB which is neither too hard nor too soft. You'll see the letters HB or the word 'Drawing' at the end of the pencil. Soft ones are called B or 2B.

Silver foil crumples and folds like paper. It is sold in kitchen rolls or you could use chocolate papers.

Tacks are short nails with large heads. They come in different lengths.

Panel pins are nails with hardly any head.

Tacks and panel pins come from a handyman's shop.

Tacking is the name for large stitches used to hold two pieces of cloth together before you do the proper stitching. Knot the end of the sewing cotton and use a contrasting colour to your cloth so that the stitches are easy to see and pull out when the work is finished.

Parts of a circle

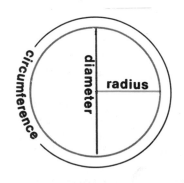

knitting wool and is usually 6-ply. 2-ply Rya rug wool is much thinner.

Stranded cotton is shiny embroidery cotton which comes with 6 strands—you usually use two or three strands at a time.

String comes in many thicknesses. The strands are twisted together. You can buy it in stationers.

Cord is like a smooth sort of string. You will find it in a haberdashery department.

Raffia is flat, like a tape. Natural buff raffia comes from garden shops. Man-made raffia from handicraft shops comes in many colours.

Glue

You can buy most kinds of glue at a stationer's shop.

School paste or paper paste is cheap and good for pasting light

things like paper. It dries clear. If you splash some on your clothes it is easy to wash out.

PVA glue is stronger than paper paste and is good for most yarn projects. You can thin it with water to use it as a varnish too. If you splash some on your clothes wash it out while it is wet: once it is dry it won't come out.

Stik'n'Fix by Bostik is one make of PVA glue.

Clear glue is very strong, but it is

also fairly expensive. It's best for gluing heavy things together, or for making spots of glue which you want to dry hard and very quickly. Bostik 1 and UHU are two well-known makes.

Rubber-based adhesive. Copydex is one make to look out for.

Sticky tape is either clear or made of brown paper with glue on one side and is sold in reels. It is useful for holding things together.

Needles

Carpet needles are very strong and sharp, sometimes curved.

Embroidery needles are sharp with a large eye.

Darning needles are like embroidery needles but longer.

Tapestry needles are blunt with a large eye.

Sewing needles are sharp and slim, with fairly small eyes.

How to use a protractor

A protractor is useful for measuring angles.

If you want to make an angle of 60°, draw a line.

Lie the protractor on the line, with its centre on the end of the line. The protractor is marked into 180 sections, called degrees. Find 60° and make a dot.

Draw a line from the dot to the end of the first line.

Tracing from this book

The trace patterns in this book are printed the *wrong* way round so that your finished picture will be the *right* way round.

You will need tracing paper, a soft pencil such as a 2B, and sticky tape. Any kind of see-through paper such as kitchen grease-proof or airmail paper will do for tracing.

1. Lay tracing paper over the pattern and fix it to the page with paper clips. Trace the outline of the pattern.

2. Turn the tracing paper over and scribble over the outline on to the paper you are using.

When you lift the tracing paper you will find an outline of the pattern on it.

If the outline is too faint, draw round it again with a pencil.

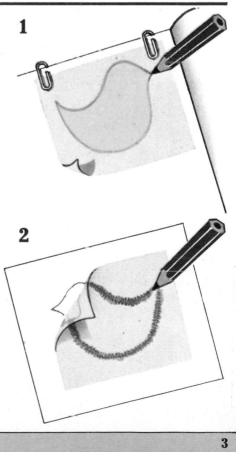

1

2

cm

Book-mark Mice

Pompons are as fun to make as they are to use. Add a pompon to last year's beret, or make these little pompon mice as bookmarks for your friends. If you give the mice heart-shaped ears, they make very special valentines.

► You will need:
☐ Half a ball of knitting wool (12.5g) in white, cream or brown
☐ A small square of felt for the ears
☐ Small beads for the eyes and nose
☐ Thin cardboard
☐ Sharp scissors
☐ A darning needle
☐ String
☐ Cup, small coin or a pair of compasses
☐ Sewing needle and cotton for beads
☐ Sticky tape

1

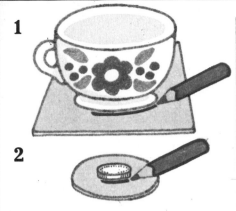

2

1. Draw two circles on the card, about 5cm in diameter. If you are using a compass, make the radius 2.5cm, otherwise draw round the base of a cup.
Cut out these two circles.

2. Draw a smaller circle in the centre of each larger circle, using a small coin. Cut out this circle to make a hole.
Cut about 20 pieces of wool, each 1 metre in length.

3

3. Put the two cardboard rings together. Wind each piece of wool in turn round the rings. Keep the end of the wool to the outer edge of the cardboard, overlapping it to hold it in place.
When the centre hole is almost filled and you can no longer push the wool through with your finger, thread the darning needle with the wool and continue winding until the hole is filled.

4

4. Now begin to snip the wool at the outside edge. Cut a few loops at a time. Don't pull on the loops as you cut them. Try to insert the point of the scissors between the two edges of the cards, so the cut wool will be all the same length.

5 string **6**

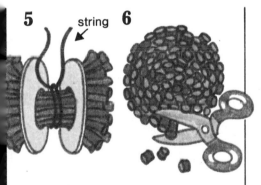

5. When all the wool is cut, tie the centre firmly with string, and make a strong knot.

6. Snip carefully through the cardboard rings from the outer edge to the inner edge and very carefully remove from the wool. Your pompon will spring into shape. Trim off any long ends. Make a second pompon for the head. You can use the same rings by taping the slits together.

7. To make the ears, trace the ear pattern on to paper. Cut it out.
8. Fold the felt in half and pin the shape to the fold. Cut round it and open out the felt.
9. Cut out the point.
10. Thread a long piece of wool through the darning needle and make a large knot at one end. Thread through the centre of one pompon, then the ears, then the other pompon. Pull them together. Tie a knot close to the second pompon, so it cannot move. The rest of the wool becomes the tail. Trim the head so that it is smaller than the body.
11. Now you can sew on small beads for the eyes and nose, threading the cotton through the centre of the pompon. Knot securely.

7

ear trace pattern

8

fold

9

10 head

ears

body

11

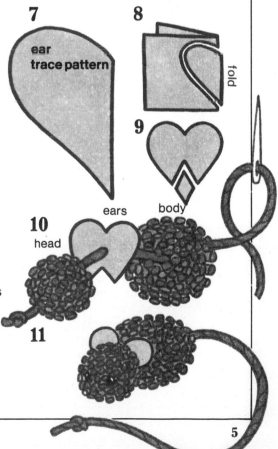

Necklace and belt

A wool-wrapped necklace or belt is a good way to use up short lengths of wool. In the photograph opposite the two inside circles are necklaces and the outside circle is a belt.

Stripy necklace

▶ You will need:
- ☐ 5mm diameter cord or clothes line, cut to the length you want the finished necklace to be
- ☐ Scraps of wool
- ☐ Darning needle
- ☐ Sewing needle and cotton

1

1. Begin wrapping 3cm from one end of the cord. Hold the end of the wool slightly down from this, then return the wool to the starting point and begin to wind it around the cord and wool end. Wind tightly and keep the wool very close together. Do not wind to the end of the wool scrap, but leave a short end.

2

2. To begin the next colour, hold the first colour end along the cord and place the second colour next to the end of the first colour. Wind over both ends and continue wrapping to within 3cm of the cord end.

3

3. To join the ends, put them together and, using a sewing needle and cotton, sew them together by running a few stitches through the centre of the cord.
Wind the wool around this join as before. To finish off, thread the end of the wool through a darning needle and pull it back through the section just completed.

1

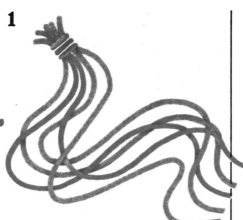

Peasant belt

For a belt you will need about 5 lengths of wool each 1 metre long and a darning needle.

1. Make a bundle with the lengths of wool and bind it at one end by wrapping it with wool.

2

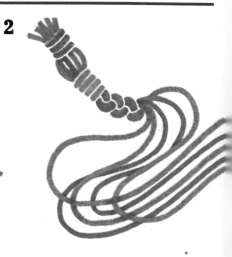

2. Repeat as you like along the length. Occasionally plait the strands of the bundle to add variety. Finish off each wrapped section with a darning needle (see step 3 of the necklace). To finish, fray the ends of the wool.

Stripy pencil holders

Don't throw away those old jars or plastic containers. Wrap them up in knitting wool and make them into colourful pots or ornaments. An empty washing-up liquid container can be transformed into a gay pencil holder, or a plain glass jam jar made into an unusual vase.

The art of wool covering comes from Mexico where dry gourds, like the ones at the top of this picture, are wrapped in brightly coloured yarns. Mexicans also make beautiful wool pictures the same way: you can try the bird picture on the next page when you have practised with a pencil holder.

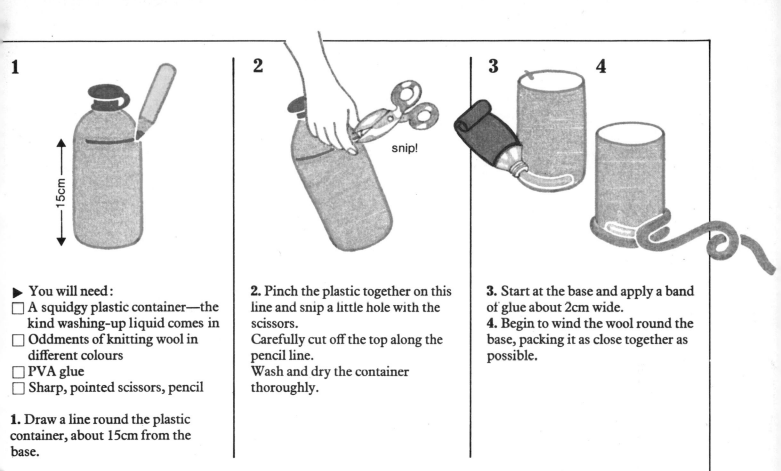

1

2

snip!

3　**4**

▶ You will need:
☐ A squidgy plastic container—the kind washing-up liquid comes in
☐ Oddments of knitting wool in different colours
☐ PVA glue
☐ Sharp, pointed scissors, pencil

1. Draw a line round the plastic container, about 15cm from the base.

2. Pinch the plastic together on this line and snip a little hole with the scissors.
Carefully cut off the top along the pencil line.
Wash and dry the container thoroughly.

3. Start at the base and apply a band of glue about 2cm wide.
4. Begin to wind the wool round the base, packing it as close together as possible.

5　**6**

7　**8**

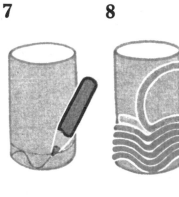

9

5. When you reach the end of the glue band, apply another band of glue. You can either continue with the colour you are using, or start on a second colour.
Continue with alternating bands of colour.
6. Finish off the top with an edging of plaited wool glued round the edge.

7. For your next pencil holder you can try a wavy line.
Draw a straight line about 2cm up from the bottom of the container.
Now draw a wavy line between the base and the straight line.
Cover 3cm with glue and lay the wool along the wavy line.
8. Continue laying wavy lines of wool, adding more bands of glue as you need to.

9. Fill in the spaces at the top and bottom by covering the plastic with glue. Starting at the outside of the space, lay down a coil of wool.
Work inwards in ever-decreasing circles until all the plastic is hidden. Snip off.

Wool pictures

Once you have made a stripy pencil holder you can go on to create a beautiful Mexican-style wool painting as a decoration for your room. For these pictures you use coloured yarns instead of ordinary paints.

This age-old art of wool collage was originally invented by the people of north-west Mexico. Their wool pictures were offered as gifts to their gods.

Before starting on your own design, choose several coloured yarns and lay them side by side to discover the most pleasing combinations.

► You will need:
- □ Double knitting wool in black
- □ Scraps of double knitting wool in red, maroon, white, turquoise, pink and orange – or your own choice of colours
- □ Thick cardboard 25cm x 12.5cm
- □ Tracing paper
- □ Pencil
- □ Sticky tape
- □ PVA glue
- □ Scissors

Trace the pattern on the facing page and transfer it on to the cardboard, holding the tracing paper in place with sticky tape. (See page 3 for how to transfer patterns.)

1. Squeeze a thin line of glue along a short part of the turquoise outline. Cut a length of turquoise wool and press it into place along the line of glue.

1

glue

2

Continue making an outline with one piece of wool all round the bird, its crest, the flower and the leaf in the same way, gluing and sticking as you go.

2. If you have to join the wool, snip off the old piece neatly and start the new piece end-on next to it.

3

3. Fill in the bird and the flower petals first with glue, then with wool in the right colours. Always fill in by working in ever-decreasing circles.

Working in the grey sections, outline all the turquoise lines with one line of black wool. Go round with another line of black wool, then fill in all the rest of the grey areas with black wool. Squeeze the glue into the spaces outside the bird and the flower. Fill in with red or maroon wool.

4. Finally, spread glue around the edges of the cardboard and finish off the picture with rows of black wool to make the frame. Trim the cardboard.

You can develop the idea further by tracing off any simple, clear-cut picture. Or you could glue a picture on to cardboard and stick the wool straight on to the picture.

4

Stitches for pictures

Chain stitch is one of the most useful stitches for making thick lines of embroidery. You can use tapestry wool, knitting yarn or two or three strands of stranded cotton. The rooster picture shown here uses two parallel lines of chain stitch for the outline, but it's a good idea to experiment first, using the little chick as a sampler.

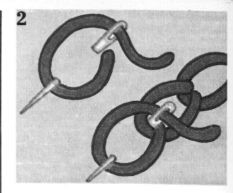

Chain stitch

Cut a piece of thread about 50cm long and tie a knot at one end. Thread it through an embroidery needle. Take the needle through a piece of scrap cloth so that the knot is on the wrong side.
1. Lie the thread on the surface of the cloth in a loop and, holding the loop with your left thumb, put the point of the needle back into the same hole from where it came.

2. Push the point of the needle out again, a little way forward and over the loop. Draw the needle and thread through gently. The thread should lie easily on the surface of the cloth, which should not be pulled out of shape by the stitch. Better to have stitches a bit too loose rather than too tight. Repeat.

3

wrong side
of cloth

Finishing off

To finish off, bring the needle
through to the wrong side so that a
little stitch holds the last chain loop
down.
Now take the thread over and under
the backs of the last three or
four stitches, making sure the
needle does not catch the cloth.
Snip off the rest of the thread.
You can use this method to finish
off all kinds of embroidery.

1

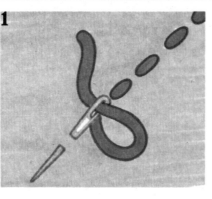

Running stitch

1. Make the stitches on the right
side of the cloth the same length
and the under ones half as long. If
you work rows of exactly matching
stitches you can make stripes.

2

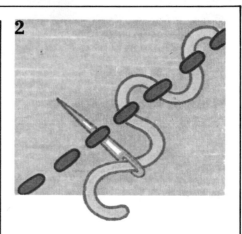

To make running stitch more
interesting you can interlace a
contrasting colour.
2. Use a tapestry needle and thread
the second colour in and out of the
running stitches without catching
the cloth.

1 **2**

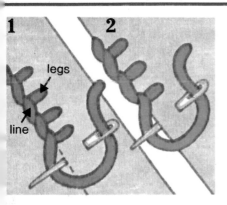

legs

line

Blanket stitch

1. Make a knot. Bring the needle up
on the line of the design. Make a
loop with the yarn and put the
needle in about 0.5cm to the right.
Bring the needle out again on the
line and pull gently through.
Repeat.
2. Blanket stitch makes a good
edging. The 'line' goes on the
outside and the 'legs' are inside.

3

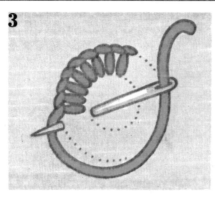

3. If you work the stitches in a
circle they will make an eye or a
button shape.

This chick makes a useful sampler
for the stitches. Trace the pattern
on to tissue paper, then pin it to a
piece of cloth and stitch through
both layers.
You could try chain stitch for the
outline of the egg and the chick;
blanket stitch for the head and
laced running stitch for the wing.
Tear away the tissue paper when
the embroidery is finished.

Rooster calendar

This rooster can be made up into a splendid calendar. But, of course, you can just make a picture.
A rooster would be fun to embroider on the front of a tee shirt too.

▶ You will need:
- ☐ Tapestry wool or 3 strands of stranded cotton in colours shown
- ☐ Tracing paper, pencil
- ☐ Needle with an eye large enough for wool and string
- ☐ Plywood 26cm x 36cm
- ☐ Hessian about 5cm larger all round than the plywood
- ☐ Sewing cotton
- ☐ Calendar with cardboard back (optional)
- ☐ Clear glue, pins, string

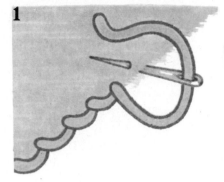

1. Oversew the edges of the hessian to prevent fraying.
Trace the rooster outline from this page on to thin tracing paper.
Pin the paper on the piece of hessian, making sure there is a 5cm border of hessian all round the pattern.
Make little running stitches along all the lines with sewing cotton.
Tear off the paper very gently.

Chain stitch the two pink circles, for the head. Now chain stitch the red outline of the body so that it touches the pink circle.
Then stitch the yellow outline.
Stitch the blue foot so that it touches the yellow line.
Complete all the other pink lines.
2. To make the eye, work round and round in a spiral.

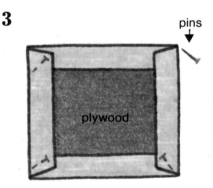

3. Lay your embroidery face down on a table. Put the plywood in the centre. Fold the hessian over the plywood and pin.
Carefully unpick all the sewing cotton running stitches.
4. Thread the needle with string and lace up the edges from side to side and from top to bottom. Pull the string evenly so the picture is not pulled out of shape. Glue a calendar to the hessian in the position shown.

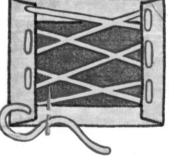

★ This pattern is different from the sort of trace pattern described on page 3. Make sure you read step 1 on the facing page carefully and check that your running stitches go through both the paper and the cloth. When you tear off the paper the running stitch lines remain on the cloth. Then you work your embroidery stitches over the running stitches.

Scatter daisies on cushions

A splash of daisy-like flowers looks very pretty on a cushion cover. You can make as many or as few daisies as you like, either scattered or arranged in a regular pattern.

The stitch used here is called daisy stitch or detached chain stitch. Once you've tried ordinary chain stitch you will see how this stitch works.

4 **5**

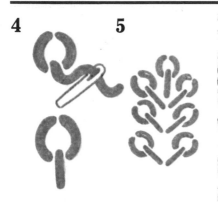

4. You can make leaf shapes by lengthening the stitch that holds the loop in place.
5. If you combine several of these stitches, you can build up bigger leaves.
Always try to keep the stitches fairly loose – don't pull them too tight or they will pucker up the cloth.

6

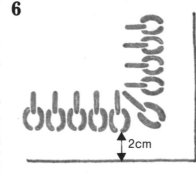

2cm

6. Leave a border 2cm all round the cloth and make a row of leaves to outline the edge of the pin cushion.
Keep the wool yarn twisted to the right so that it does not unravel.
Fill in the spaces with leaves and smaller flowers if you like.

7 **8**

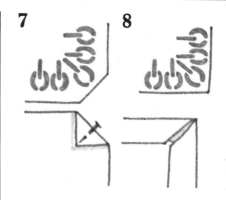

7. Fold all four corners in diagonally so that the tip of the corner leaf just touches the fold. Pin in place.
8. Fold the edges of the cloth so the row of leaves is at the edge. Pin and tack.
Fold and tack the material for the back in the same way.

Pin cushion

The best kind of cloth to try out stitches on is called Binca. It is woven in blocks of cotton strands separated by holes. Hessian is good too. If you try out your stitches on a little square of cloth, you can turn it into a pretty pin cushion.

▶ You will need:
- ☐ 2 pieces of cloth 12cm x 12cm
- ☐ Pair of old laddered tights
- ☐ Scraps of tapestry wool
- ☐ Tapestry needle

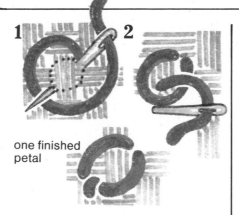

one finished petal

Thread the needle with tapestry wool and tie a knot at one end. Bring the needle through to the middle of the right side of one of the pieces of cloth.
1. Make a loop with the thread, push the needle back through the cloth at the same spot it came out and bring the point out again over the loop.
Pull the thread through gently.
2. Make another tiny stitch to hold the loop in place.

3. If you want to make a whole flower, take the needle round and start another little petal next to the one you have just made. Look at the cushion on the left: you'll notice that some of the flowers have four petals, some have six, some have eight.
The squares of the Binca cloth or the hessian help you to keep the daisy shapes regular.

9

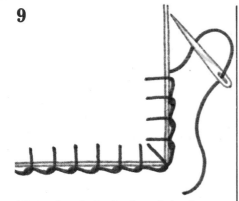

Pin and tack the back and the front together, wrong sides facing.
9. Sew the back and front together around three sides with blanket stitch.
Push in the pair of tights and blanket stitch the fourth side together. Carefully remove all tacking stitches.

The daisy cushion cover

Once you have made a pin cushion you can go on to create a bigger cushion for a chair, like the one in the photograph. If you make up your own pattern you needn't cover all the cloth with daisies.

▶ You will need:
- ☐ Two pieces of cloth 35cm x 35cm.
- ☐ Tapestry wool in lots of different colours
- ☐ Tapestry needle
- ☐ Cushion pad 32cm x 32cm, or an old cushion of this size
- ☐ Graph paper
- ☐ Coloured crayons

It's a good idea to work out your design on graph paper with coloured crayons, to see the effect.

If you are using Binca cloth, you can make each square of the graph paper represent one of the Binca squares. If you are using hessian, a square can represent two or three threads.
Then follow steps 1–9 of 'Try it first'. Put in the cushion pad instead of the tights in step 9.

Practise with a pair of thick knitting needles or garden sticks. Bumpy twigs or differently sized sticks will change the look of your stars, so will different yarns.
The sticks are first lashed together then the star can be wound in two different ways, either showing the shape of the sticks or covering them completely. Always pull the wool tightly so that the sticks stay in place.
The star in the photograph on the left is mostly wound as in step 2, but the blue band is wound as in step 4.

▶ You will need:
☐ Two sticks, each about 25cm long and 5mm thick
☐ Oddments of 3-ply wool in brilliant colours

Make your lucky star

With oddments of knitting wool woven round two sticks you can make pretty stars to hang on the wall. In parts of South America one is made for each year of a child's life for luck.
Sometimes the age of a child is also represented by the number of colours used.

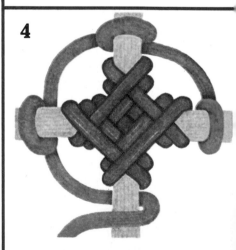

This way of wrapping shows the shape of the sticks on the front.
4. Wind the yarn over the top of the right hand stick and around the underside again.
Now wind yarn under and over the top stick, under and over the left stick.
Continue winding under and over all round until you change colours.

1

Start by lashing the sticks together. Lay one stick across the other. Lay one end of the yarn over the centre. Hold the sticks together with the thumb and index finger of your left hand, trapping the yarn with your thumb.
1. Criss-cross the yarn over the centre from right to left until it is covered. Knot the yarn at back but do not cut it.

2

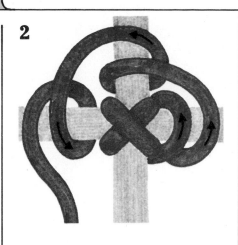

This way of wrapping covers the sticks completely on the front of the star.
2. Bring the yarn from underneath, wind it round the top of the right hand stick, under it, then over to the next upright stick.
Wind the yarn over, then round again to the next stick. Continue in the same way.

3

This is the method to use when you want to change colours.
3. On the wrong side cut off the yarn, leaving a tail 5cm long. Loop the tail once around the stick and tuck the end under the loop, pulling tightly.
Tie on the new colour with a double knot very close to the stick.

5

5. To finish a star, knot the yarn around the stick and cut off neatly. You can leave your star as it is, with the ends of the arms neatly wrapped in wool, or trim it in various ways. Pompons, feathers, bows, seashells and beads can all be used as ornaments.

Toothpick stars

You can make tiny stars like the ones on the right with very thin wool or stranded cotton on wooden toothpicks. One star has tiny sequin birds attached to the ends of the arms, while the other is trimmed with buttons. Stars like these could be grouped in a mobile or they could dangle from a Christmas tree.

Rag-bag table mats

Almost everyone has made plaits at some time – plaits of hair, plaits of wool. But if you use cut-up strips of cloth you can turn the plaits into all sorts of useful things like table mats, or braids for clothes or a rug for a doll's house. The easiest kind of cloth to use is cotton—you could use rag-bag scraps from worn-out summer dresses or blouses.

7

Loop the T end over a hook or a door handle.
7. Bring the left-hand strip over the centre strip and the right-hand strip over that. Continue plaiting, keeping the folded edges towards the centre of the plait. As you finish a strip, join on a new one as in steps 4 and 5, until the strip is about one metre long.
Make another strip the same length.

8

Now to lace the strips together. Thread a tapestry needle with two strands of sewing cotton.
8. Draw the needle through the loop of one plait, then through the facing loop of the other plait. Go on to the end. Knot the ends together – and you have a belt. You can make it wider by adding more plaits.

A table mat

As well as the things listed under 'Try it first' you will need a sewing needle, a crochet hook and enough scraps of pretty cotton cloth to add up to about 1 metre x 50cm. This will make one table mat about 25cm in diameter.

If you choose scraps in similar colours—such as reds, oranges and pinks—the mat will look very subtle. If you use a mixture of colours the effect will be more like a patchwork.

Start by plaiting the cotton strips as in 'Try it first' steps 1–7. When your plait is about 60cm long you can start sewing it together.

plaiting

Before going on to making coils for things like mats, it's a good idea to practise with a few straight strips first. If they work out well, you can turn them into a colourful tie belt for your jeans.

▶ You will need:
- ☐ Scraps of cotton cloth
- ☐ Scissors
- ☐ Sewing needle
- ☐ Tapestry needle
- ☐ Three pieces of cardboard each about 10cm x 5cm

Start by cutting or tearing the cloth up into strips about 2.5cm wide.

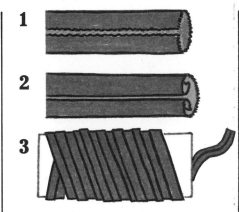

1. Fold the strips so that the cut edges meet in the middle of the wrong side of the cloth.
2. Bring the folded edges together and make a flat strip with both cut edges inside. Press the fold flat with your finger, and wind the strip around a piece of cardboard.
3. Make two more sets of strips, and wind them round cardboard too.

4. Unfold a few centimetres of the cut edges of two strips and put the ends at right angles. Join the two pieces together by sewing across the corner diagonally. Snip off the corner.
5. Straighten the joined strips and flatten out the seam with your finger-nail.
6. Attach another folded strip with a few stitches, to make a T.

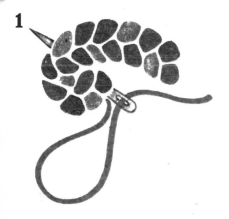

Thread a sewing needle with two strands of sewing cotton.
1. Start coiling up the plait and darn through the centre of the coil from side to side, as invisibly as possible.

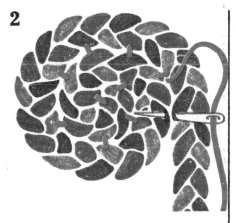

2. Sew the outside loops of the coil to the piece you are joining on. Pull the thread through gently until the two pieces lie next to each other. Keep laying the mat on a table to make sure it is flat. If it becomes hat-shaped, you are probably pulling the thread too tight.

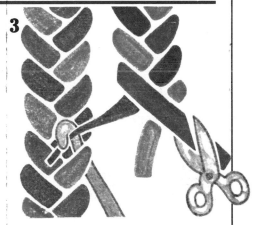

When the mat is the right size, snip off the ends of the strips so they taper a bit. This way the end will not look bumpy. Weave the ends into the outer coil of the mat.
3. If you have a crochet hook you can use it to tug the strips through the next-door loops.
Stitch in the ends as invisibly and as securely as possible.

Lots of braids

Weave bright and beautiful braids with your fingers! It's as simple as that – once you have mastered the art of finger weaving. The technique is just like plaiting, except that you are using lots of lengths instead of only three. Your fingers weave each length in turn over and under the rest of the wool to make a strip of braid.

The yarn

You can use double knitting wool, tapestry wool or rug wool. Rug wool is easy to handle and grows quickly, but you will need to use longer pieces of wool than are suggested in the instructions. Contrasting colours produce a bold effect; matching colours a more subtle effect.

The knob

Anything you can loop the wool over and pull on will do – a door handle, a drawer handle, a hook or a knob on the top of a chair.

1

For this practice piece, each length of wool should be a different colour. It will make a fine book mark.

▶ You will need:
- [ ] 4 lengths of wool each about 1 metre long
- [ ] Long pencil or thick stick
- [ ] Knob

1. Loop the four lengths of wool over a knob and knot them together.

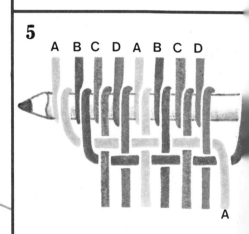

5

A B C D A B C D

A

5. Now start your right-hand edge. Bring length A down and weave it under or over length B (whichever completes the weaving sequence). Give A a good tug, then push it parallel to the other vertical threads with your finger as in step 4.

2

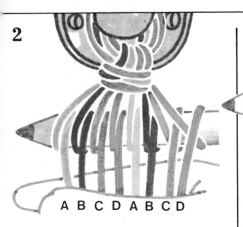

A B C D A B C D

2. Wind each length in turn around a pencil, about 5cm below the knot. The way you arrange the colours at this stage will determine your pattern. Our illustration shows four colours—A, B, C, D; A, B, C and D. Hold the rest of the wool towards you in your right hand about 10cm below the pencil.

3

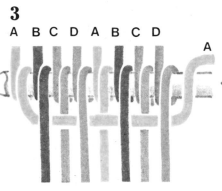

A B C D A B C D   A

3. Working from left to right, pick up length A with your left hand and pass it under length B, over length C, under length D and so on until you have woven in and out of all seven lengths.
Pull length A parallel with the pencil and tuck it over the right-hand end of the pencil.

4

A B C D A B C D   A B

4. Take length B and weave it under length C and so on until all the lengths have been crossed. Pull length B parallel with the pencil and, with the forefinger of your left hand, push it up close to the pencil. This will help to keep the pattern even and straight.
Tuck length B over the pencil.

6

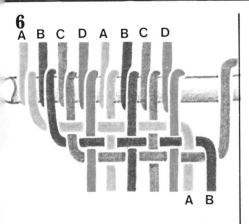

A B C D A B C D

A B

6. Pick up length C and weave it under length D, over the next thread and so on until all the threads have been crossed, including length A which is now on the extreme right.
Continue the right edge by bringing down length B to complete the weaving sequence and tuck length C over the pencil.

7

Continue weaving each thread from the left to the right, following the under-and-over sequence and making the edge on the right.
Sort out the threads as you go along so they do not get tangled.
Always pull the right edge firmly to prevent it from curving.
7. After several rows you will see a pattern developing!

8

8. When you are about 5cm from the end knot pairs of threads together then straighten out the loose ends. Trim this fringe straight.

Remove the woven braid from the knob, pull out the pencil, untie the knot and cut through the loop.
Make pairs of knots and trim.
Your book mark is ready.

From head bands to guitar straps

It's such fun experimenting with different colour combinations, stripe patterns and numbers of lengths. Once you have followed the steps in 'Try it first' you are ready to start making beautiful hair bands, bracelets and hat bands. When you can work happily without getting in a tangle, you can go on to making longer things like belts, bag handles and guitar straps.

Numbers of lengths

It is best not to use more than 24 lengths at a time – the wool can get in an awful tangle when you use more.

Amounts of wool

How long each piece of wool needs to be depends on the thickness of the wool and the width of the braid. You will usually be safe if you multiply by four. For example, to make a head band 50cm long, cut pieces of wool 2 metres long and loop these over the hook to make two lengths of 1 metre each.

A hat band, like the one in the photograph above, makes a splendid present for a grown-up. Measure round the hat first, then multiply by four to find out how long the pieces of wool should be. This hat band was made with the 18-strand ripple stripe pattern shown on the right.

Ripple stripes

If you make each stripe of colour only two threads wide, it gives the pattern a ripply look. The numbers in the diagram below tell you how many lengths of wool in each colour to wind round your pencil – there are 18 lengths altogether. The braid will look more interesting if you make one stripe a bit wider than the rest.

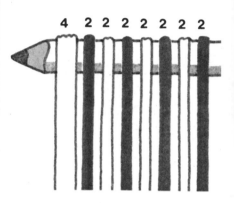

Candy stripes

Big, broad bands of colours look
very effective too.
The diagram below shows a
different way to arrange 18 lengths,
this time with three colours.

Chalk stripes

You can emphasize stripes of colour
by outlining each stripe with a
black or a white line. (If you have
two white threads on the left
you do not need to put another
pair of white threads on the right.)
Try reversing the way you weave
this time. If you work from right
to left you'll find the stripes will
go that way too.

Wavy lines

Arrange four colours in the order
shown – with the same colour on
the right and the left.
Follow steps 1–7 of 'Try it first'
until the centre stripes touch the
right-hand edge. Now pick up
the thread on the far right and
weave it across to the left.
Continue weaving from right to
left until the centre stripes reach
the left edge. Now go back to
weaving from left to right.

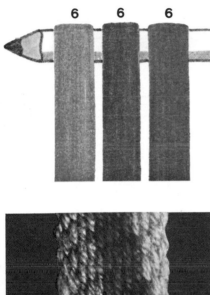

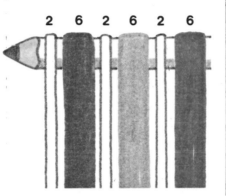

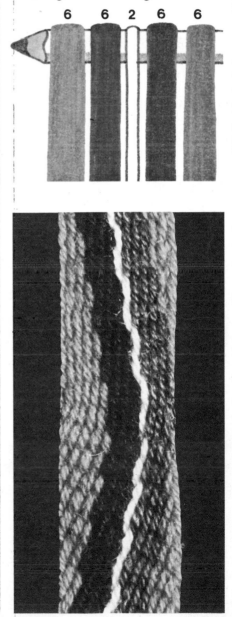

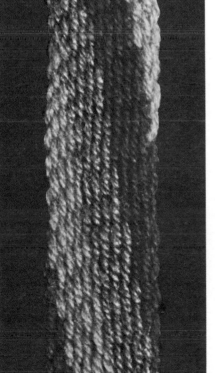

Woven braids and bags

Weaving is rather like darning a sock – lots of threads are stretched one way and another thread is interlaced backwards and forwards until a piece of cloth is formed. A loom is needed to hold the threads tight enough for weaving and you will find there are many things around the house which will act as suitable looms.

Can you guess what loom was used for the shoulder bag in the photograph? (you'll find the answer on page 29.)

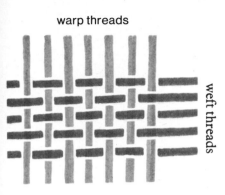

warp threads

weft threads

Warp and weft threads

This close-up shows how woven threads are interlaced.

The up-and-down threads are always called the warp. Threads woven in and out of the warp are called the weft. (The easy way to remember is you *weave* the *weft*.) Almost any kind of yarn can be used for the weft threads, but the warp threads should be strong, and not too fluffy or stretchy.

Start with a braid

A loom is any kind of frame on which you can stretch the warp. You can use the legs of a chair or a table, an embroidery frame or a picture frame, even a plastic clothes horse or the banisters! Try making a braid like the one in the photograph on page 29 first. If you use a pair of chair legs or an embroidery frame you can weave a braid long enough to make a book mark or even a hat band. A plastic clothes horse may be long enough to make a belt or a shoulder strap.

▶ You will need:
- [ ] Some sort of loom
- [ ] Corrugated cardboard
- [ ] Sticky tape
- [ ] Ball of jute garden twine
- [ ] 2 carpet needles
- [ ] Fork
- [ ] Scissors

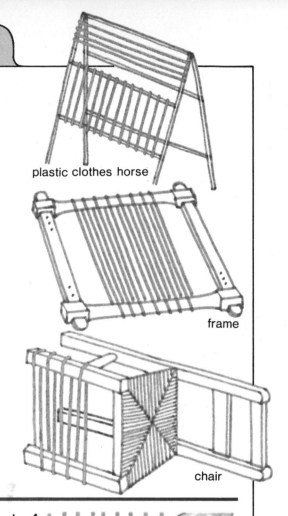

plastic clothes horse

frame

chair

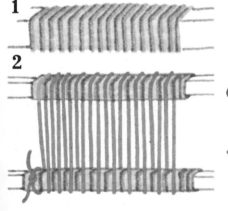

1. Tape some corrugated cardboard to the loom to help you space the warp threads evenly.

2. Tie the twine to one bar of the loom and wind the warp in one continuous length in a figure of eight until you have 19 warp threads with one thread in each groove. Do not let the warp threads cross. To finish, knot the twine to the frame.

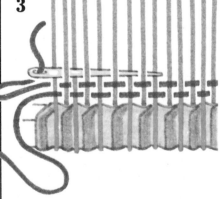

Thread one carpet needle with a length of twine about 90cm long. This will be your weft thread.

3. Leave about 8cm of tail, then start weaving in and out of the warp with the carpet needle. Pull the twine through, then weave back in the opposite direction going under all the threads you went over the first time, and over the ones you went under.

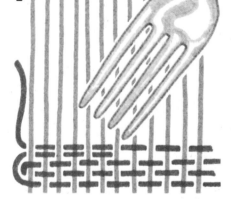

4. Use the fork to press down the weft threads gently but firmly. Thread the tail through the needle and weave it across the third row with the weft. Cut off the rest of the tail.

5

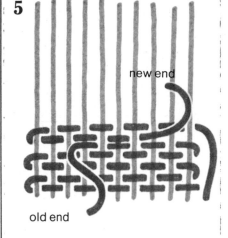

new end

old end

Weave seven more rows, pushing each row down with the fork.
Take care not to pull the weft too tightly at the edges or the band will curve or become wiggly.

5. If you need to join a new weft thread, overlap the new end and the old one. Try not to get knots in either the warp or the weft.

6

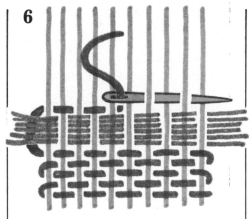

6. Take six lengths of twine each one metre long and thread them through the other needle.
Weave one row, leaving the ends of the six threads in a tuft. Push down. Leave the six strands hanging and pick up the single strand. Weave a row with one strand.
Weave a row with six strands.

7

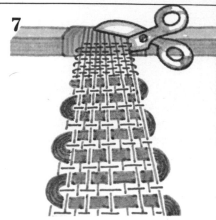

Weave alternate lengths with one strand and six strands.
Finish with 10 rows of one-strand weaving and weave in the end.

7. Cut the warp threads near to the loom frame. Trim to make a stubby fringe at each end.
Does your braid look like the one in the photograph on the right?

2

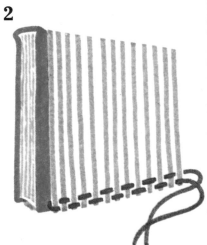

2. Thread the carpet needle with wool in the main colour. Starting at the right-hand side, leave a 30cm 'tail'. Weave to the left and back again, finishing with another tail 30cm long.

3

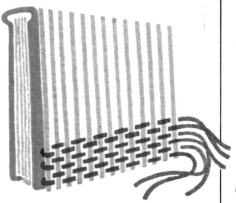

3. Continue for about 2cm, then weave in a stripe of a different colour, always leaving tails.
Weave right round the book in this way, including the spine and the front.
Slide the book out.

4

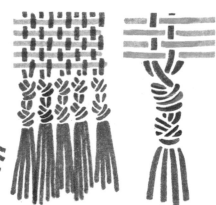

4. Join the bag at the bottom by knotting each pair of weft threads twice with a pair from the opposite side.

A shoulder bag

The bag in the photograph on page 26 was woven using a book as a loom. The shoulder strap was plaited and sewn to the sides. Four-ply rug wool is best, but you could use chunky knitting wool instead. Or use scraps of contrasting knitting wool for different-coloured stripes.

▶ You will need:
- ☐ Ball of twine
- ☐ 125g of 4-ply wool in main colour
- ☐ 4·5m each of wool in three contrasting colours
- ☐ Book, about 25cm x 20cm
- ☐ Carpet needle
- ☐ Darning needle and sewing cotton
- ☐ Scissors

1

1. Wind the twine round and round the book. Knot the two ends firmly to the threads next to them. This is the warp.

To make the shoulder strap cut 18 strands of wool, each 1·5 metres long.

5. Plait nine strands to make one side, then plait the other nine for the second side.
Knot each plait twice at the bottom, then knot them together at the top.

6. Use the darning needle and thread to stitch the plaits to the sides of the bag, starting from the bottom. This should leave about 25cm each side for the handle.
Of course, you could make a woven braid like the one in the 'Try it first' steps if you prefer.

5

6

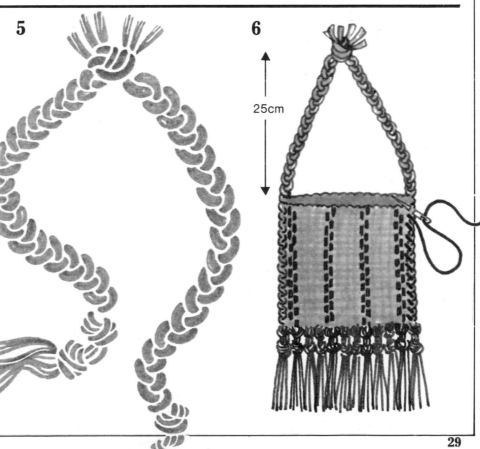

25cm

Shaggy rya cushions

Once upon a time shaggy rugs, with long-haired pile like this cushion, were used as cosy knee rugs for sleighs in Finland. This long shaggy pile was called 'rya' and you can easily copy the effect. Cushions made this way grow thick and fast, and you can use vivid splashes of plain colours, as well as subtle mixtures.

3 **4** **5** **6** **7** **8**

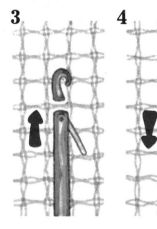

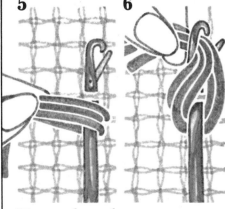

To make a knot

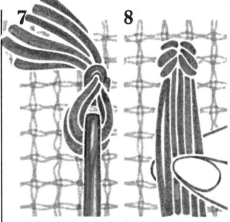

It's easier to use a latch hook if you practise first without yarn.
3. Take the hook and slip it up under a weft thread of the canvas so that the latch lies downwards.
4. Push it up so that the latch goes right through then pull the hook down again. The latch moves upwards to stop the hook being caught in the canvas.

5. Fold three cut lengths of wool in half. Loop them round the neck of the latch hook below the latch. Hold the ends of the wool between the thumb and the first finger of your left hand and push the hook under the first of the weft threads.
6. Turn the hook a little to the right, open the latch and place the ends of the wool loosely into the hook.

7. Pull the hook under the weft and through the loop of wool (the latch closes to hold the wool).
8. Pull the ends of the wool tightly to make the knot firm.

You will need:
- Rug canvas 30cm wide, 40cm long
- 14 packs of 2-ply rya wool: 6 packs of turquoise, 4 of grass green and 4 of violet—or your own choice of colours
- Latch hook
- Piece of backing cloth 35cm x 35cm
- Cushion pad 30cm x 30cm
- Darning needle
- Some knitting wool

1. Rug canvas comes in various widths and you can buy it as narrow as 30cm wide. It should have 10 holes to every 7·5cm. Most canvas is marked in squares 10 holes by 10 holes. If yours is not, use a felt-tipped pen to mark it into squares.

Two-ply rya rug wool is usually sold in packs of 168 pieces which are cut into 18cm lengths.

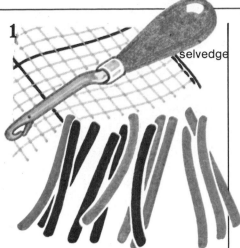

The latch hook is for knotting the wool to the canvas.

With rya wool you work with three strands of wool for every knot. You can use three lengths all of the same colour, or you can make subtle mixtures by using two lengths of one colour and one length of another colour.

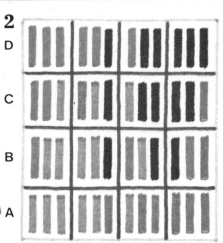

2. Your piece of canvas should be marked into 16 squares. You will be making each square on the canvas a different colour – some plain, some mixed. The chart above shows you how many lengths of each colour to use in the latch hook for the knots in each square.

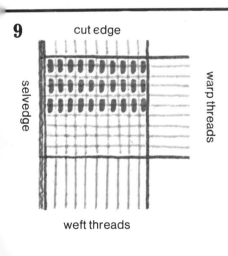

9. Practise first by doing two rows in the left-hand square of section B. (Check what mixture of colours you should be using for the square.) With rya yarn you only make knots on every alternate weft thread. Start at the left of the square and work across the weft. Make a knot in every hole. Leave a weft thread. Make another row of knots.

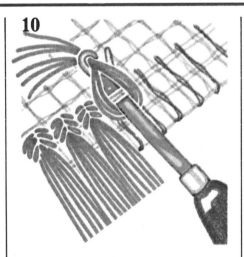

When you have got the knack of making knots, fill in section A.

10. Turn about 5cm of the cut edges *upwards* and fold the edges over so the holes match the holes below. Using the right colours for the square, hook through both layers of weft threads so you 'tie' the cut edge down.

Work the rows right across from left to right, changing colours as you move into the next square. Remember to leave a weft thread, then make another row of knots through both layers of canvas. Work your way up the canvas. (If your first practice knots turn out to be on the wrong rows, undo them and make new knots.) When you come to section D, turn up the cut edge and knot through both layers as in step 10.

When the canvas is completely covered, turn *under* the selvedge edges. Sew them to the back of the canvas with needle and wool.

Prepare the backing cloth in the way described on page 17, steps 7–9 (put in a cushion pad though, not tights!) Blanket stitch the front and the back together with wool in the same way.

Rings knots mats and frames

The mat, scarf ring and ball-shaped knots in the photograph on the left are all made with one method of circular plaiting which is called a Turk's head. Once you have got the hang of this basic method you can adapt the scarf ring to make napkin rings or even use thick rope to turn the little mat into a doormat!

3

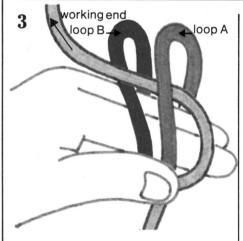

3. Turn your hand round a bit and tuck the working end under loop A and over loop B, from right to left.

4

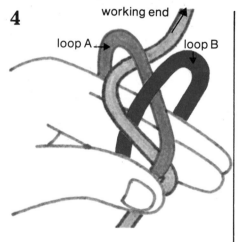

4. Cross loop B over loop A and tuck the working end from left to right under A and over B.

5

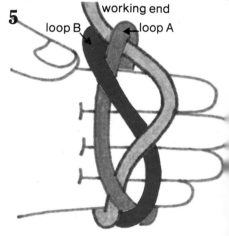

5. Turn the circle a little more and cross loop B over A, then pass the working end under A and over B to the left. Each strand has now been wound in and out three times.

Bear in mind all the time that you are making a circular plait. Anything you make is simply smaller, larger, rounder or flatter. The size is set by the size of the basic loop, which needs to be a bit bigger than the finished project.

The Turk's head

It helps the first time you make a circular plait to mark the cord with colours so that you can remember which strand is which. (Once you have succeeded, you will find you do not need to mark them any more).

▶ You will need :
- [ ] 3 metres beige or white cord at least 3mm thick (this is enough for a scarf ring, napkin ring or bracelet).
- [ ] Blue and red felt-tipped pens or crayons
- [ ] Clear glue, scissors

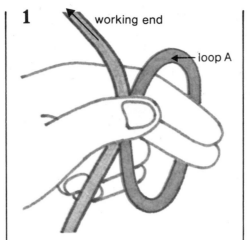

1. Loop the cord around the fingers of your left hand so that one third hangs down. The rest is called the working end. Cross this working end to the left and hold it under your thumb. This makes basic loop A; colour this blue.

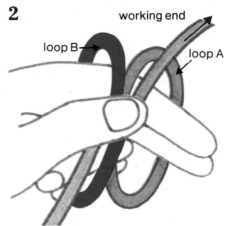

2. Pass the working end round your fingers again to form loop B and hold this loop under your thumb too. Colour loop B red. (Both these loops need to be a bit bigger than the size of your finished project.)

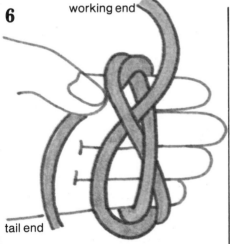

6. To work the second round, take the working end and feed it back into the knot under the loop from which the tail end comes out. Keeping to the right hand side, weave the working end round again, alongside the first round, following the windings until you have two strands all round.

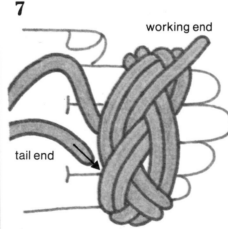

7. To add a third round, weave the tail end around the circle, working in the reverse direction until there are three strands all round.

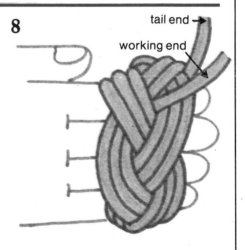

8. To finish, cut the two ends so that they are hidden behind the windings. Tuck them in neatly and add a dab of glue to prevent them from unravelling.

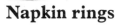

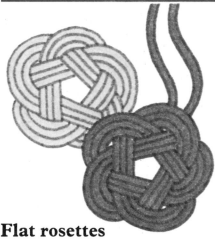

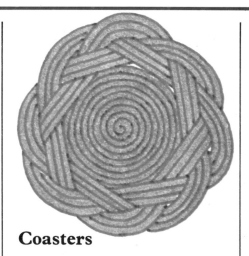

Napkin rings

Work the Turk's head round a piece of cardboard tube about 6cm in diameter. Slip the ring off the tube, even out the windings if necessary and then glue it to the cardboard tube to keep it firm. Trim the ends and tuck them in neatly.

Bracelets

Cut a strip of thin cardboard about 4cm wide and glue the ends together to make a ring the size you want the bracelet to be. Make the Turk's head over the ring in the same way as for the napkin ring. You will have to make more windings in and out as you are working round a larger circle. Remove the cardboard ring.

Scarf rings

To make a Turk's head scarf ring wind the cord around the two or three middle fingers of your left hand.
The hole through the middle should be big enough to put a finger through when you have finished the rounds. If the hole is getting too small, two rounds will look fine.

Flat rosettes

After you have wound the first round of the Turk's head it is quite easy to press the circle flat on a table. Then simply carry on working the next rounds flat. Finish off the ends as usual. You can use these rosettes as little mats or as trimmings.

Coasters

You can turn a Turk's head into a coaster by working it over a cardboard ring of the right size, in the same way as for a bracelet. Flatten it out and glue it to a round piece of cardboard. Fill in the central hole with a coil of cord glued in place (work this from the outside inwards).

Picture frames

An unusual picture frame could be made in a similar way to the coaster, with a larger Turk's head circle glued to a cardboard base. Leave a space wide enough to slip the picture in. This one has only two rounds of plaiting.
You will need about 4 metres of cord for an 11cm diameter frame.

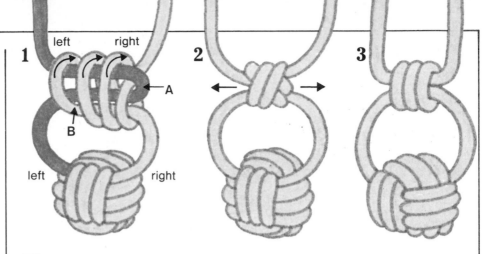

Ball knots

These are quite hard to do!
Make a Turk's head in the same
way as the scarf ring, taking the
working end once to the left, once
to the right and again to the left.
Make one or two more rounds. To
turn it into a ball, you have to push
the fullness in each loop round and
pull out the working end and the
tail, bit by bit.

Tie-ons

Tie-ons are useful for tying on to
anything you do not want to lose,
like scissors or your best pen.
Start by making a ball knot in the
middle of the cord.
1. Hold one end of the cord in your
left hand and make loop A. Hold
the other end of the cord in your
right hand and lie part B along the
loop. Wind the right end three
times over loop A and B. Bring the
end round again and thread it
through the end of the loop.
2. Pull both left cords with your left
hand and both right cords with your
right hand until the knot tightens
up.
3. Turn it over and you will
discover a neat three-ring knot.

Pots and jars

Coiled cord can transform a plain
glass storage jar, yet the contents
can still be seen if you leave some of
the glass uncovered. You don't have
to glue all the cord, just the
beginning and the end.
Cover the lid by coiling from the
outside inwards, then the sides.
Trim with a flat rosette in a
different colour.

Another idea for a present is to
dress up a plastic plant pot with
a cover of coiled cord. Finish the
rim with a plaited Turk's head
border (work it round the pot to
get the size right).

Pictures with angles

Geometry suddenly becomes fun when you're making pictures with pins. A row of straight lines magically turn themselves into unusual curved shapes and, once you have mastered one basic shape, you will want to go on and invent your own pictures. You can experiment with different backgrounds and yarns too.
The picture in the photograph above is made with green yarn, a zigzag of little copper nails and a cork floor tile.

1

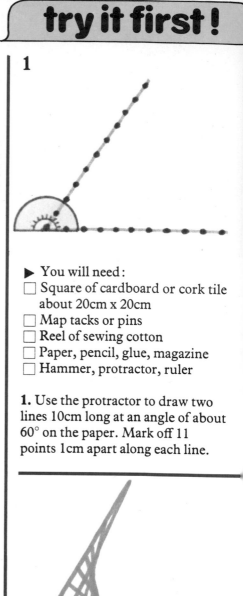

▶ You will need:
☐ Square of cardboard or cork tile about 20cm x 20cm
☐ Map tacks or pins
☐ Reel of sewing cotton
☐ Paper, pencil, glue, magazine
☐ Hammer, protractor, ruler

1. Use the protractor to draw two lines 10cm long at an angle of about 60° on the paper. Mark off 11 points 1cm apart along each line.

You can either leave your design as a piece of pure geometry or turn it into a picture.
A boat shape under one triangle will turn it into a sailing boat. Or two triangles and a few felt pen lines can become a seagull.

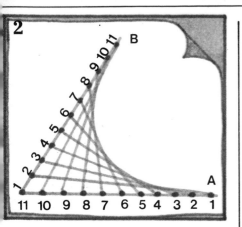

2. Number the points as shown. Join the dots as shown with pencil lines: point 1A to point 1B, point 2A to point 2B and so on. See how the lines turn into curves! Now pin the paper to the square of cardboard or cork and put it onto an old magazine. Gently hammer pins in place through the points on the paper.
Tear off the paper.

Tie sewing cotton to pin 1A with a double knot (don't break it off from the reel as you must only use one length of yarn for the complete threading).
3. Wind yarn from pin 1A round 1B.
4. Go round pins 1B and 2B as shown. Then go from 2B to 2A, then from 3A to 3B and so on. Always wind round pins as shown. Keep the yarn tight, in a continuous length to the end. Double knot the yarn to the last pin (11B) and snip off. Finish with a dab of glue.

If you draw the same angle, with points 0·5cm apart this time, you will see that the curve looks much smoother. The more pins you have, the better the curve—the important thing to remember is that they must be evenly spaced.

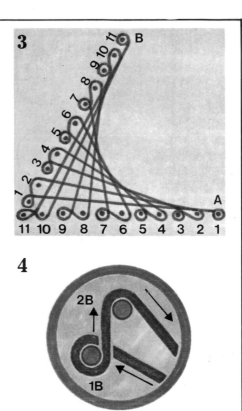

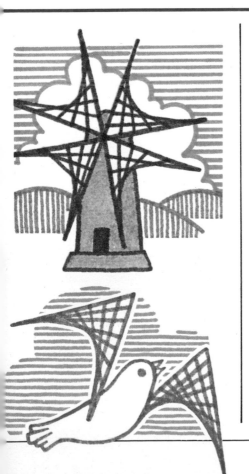

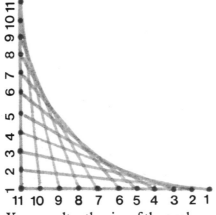

You can alter the size of the angle to change the shape of the curve. The diagram above shows the kind of curve two lines at right angles will produce.

To find out exactly how much yarn you need for a design, all you have to do is draw the design first, measure all the lines, add them up and add 20cm extra to allow for starting and finishing off.

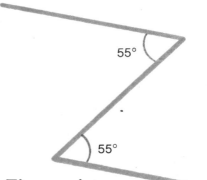

Zigzag picture

The photograph on the opposite page is made with two angles of 55° in a zigzag. Make one angle first, then the other one, sharing the centre line of the zigzag for both windings.

Diamond and circles

Diamond pictures

You can make your pictures look very professional if you use a panel of soft board or a polystyrene tile about 1·5cm thick and cover it with cloth.

The one in this photograph is covered with green felt, teamed with copper tacks and copper-coloured crochet yarn.

▶ You will need:
- ☐ Board or tile about 17cm x 32cm or 30cm x 60cm
- ☐ Piece of hessian or felt 5cm larger all round than the board
- ☐ Nails, tacks or panel pins about 2cm long
- ☐ Ball of yarn
- ☐ Sheet of paper same size as the board
- ☐ Pencil, hammer, glue, protractor
- ☐ Ruler or strip of wood

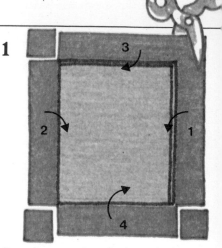

1

Start by covering the board with the cloth.

1. Lay the cloth on the table and put the board on top.
Cut away the corners of the cloth.
Glue round the edges of the board.
Lift the cloth over the sides of the board, pressing it down and pulling it tight.

Making circles

This is the way to position pins at equal distances around the circumference of a circle.
You will need all the things listed for the Diamond picture plus a pair of compasses and a nail with a large head.

1. Draw a large circle with a pair of compasses on a piece of paper. Draw in the diameter.
2. Using a protractor, mark off every 5°. Use a ruler to join these points from the centre of the circle to the circumference.
3. Cover the board with felt or hessian as before. Pin on the paper. Hammer a large-headed nail into the centre of the circle.

2

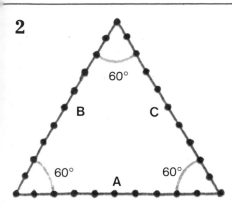

60°

B   C

60°   60°

A

2. Draw an equal-sided triangle on paper (one with every angle 60°). You can make each side 10cm long, or 20cm long, depending on the size of your board.
Mark off each side accurately with 11 or 21 equally spaced points.
Draw another triangle, using side A of the top triangle. Mark off as before.
Pin the paper pattern to the cloth on the board.

3. Hammer the nails or tacks into the board, following the paper pattern.
To keep all the nails the same height you can use a ruler or a strip of wood. Just hammer each nail in place until the head is level with the wood. Check that the nails don't go right through the board!

Remove the paper pattern.
4. Following 'Try it first' step 3, thread the design for the top triangle first. Do one angle at a time. Then thread the lower triangle, sharing the nails on line A of the top triangle.

3

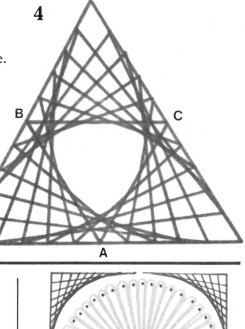

4

B   C

A

1

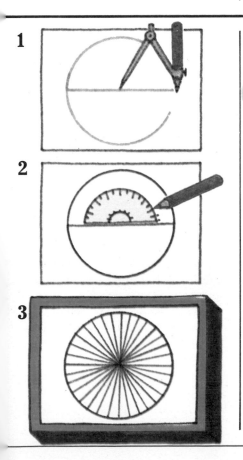

2

3

4

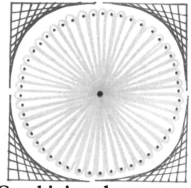

5

4. Hammer tacks or nails through all the points on the circumference. Tie the yarn on to the large nail. Wind the yarn around any nail on the circumference and bring it back to the centre.
5. Wind the yarn around the next nail on the circumference, working clockwise, until all the nails are used up. The large head on the centre nail should prevent the yarn from slipping off.

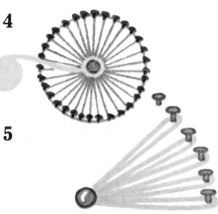

Combining shapes

Right angles and circles combine to make beautiful patterns.
See how many patterns and pictures you can think of that combine angles, triangles, circles and semi-circles.
Or you can make pictures using circles for things like wheels, a semi-circle for a sunrise, or a fan or the radiator of a car.

Witch doctor masks

It's worth making a try-out funny nose first. Then you can either tie it on with a piece of elastic and give everyone a fright, or keep it to stick on a proper mask later.

▶ You will need:
☐ Ball of string or hank of raffia
☐ Egg cup
☐ Silver foil
☐ PVA glue
☐ Mixing cup for glue
☐ Tablespoon
☐ Elastic thread
☐ Old newspaper

A mask like this can disguise you completely, yet you can see through it quite easily. It is made from coarse string wound round a shape and then coated with glue to make it stiff enough to stay in the shape. When the glue is dry you can stick on all kinds of decorations like beady eyes, plaited ears and wild hair. You can use raffia instead of string: it's lighter to wear and cheaper too.

1. Find a plastic bucket or a large bowl. Try it on and see if it fits. If it is large enough to slip on easily you can use it for making your mask. The base must be the widest part so that you can pull the bucket out easily when the mask is made.

40

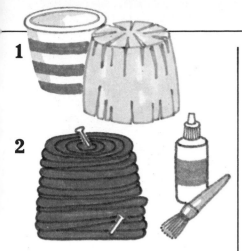

1. Cover an egg cup with silver foil.
2. Pin and coil string or raffia round it.
Mix a spoonful of PVA glue with two spoonfuls of water. Brush on and leave to dry overnight. Paint on more glue mixture.

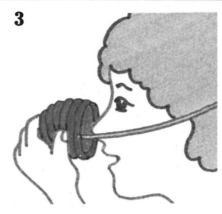

When it is dry you will see that the coiled string or raffia keeps its shape when you take it off the egg cup.
3. Thread the elastic through the edge of the nose shape, take it round your head and tie it to the other side. Try not to make the elastic too tight or it may pull the nose apart.

Witch doctor masks

Sketch your mask with crayons on paper before you begin. Try several designs to see the effect but keep the shape of the mask fairly plain as you cannot force string or hessian into difficult shapes. Ask a friend to help you with the winding.

▶ You will need :
- [ ] Ball of thick sisal string or a hank of raffia
- [ ] Plastic bucket or large bowl
- [ ] PVA glue for stiffening
- [ ] Mixing cup for glue
- [ ] Rubber-based glue for coating the inside and sticking on the features
- [ ] Brushes, pins, safety pins
- [ ] Silver foil
- [ ] Cardboard for base and features
- [ ] Beads, buttons, raffia
- [ ] Fabric dyes or coloured inks
- [ ] Apron, old newspaper

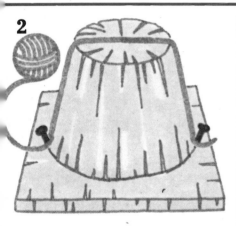

2. Cover the bucket with foil, also cover a square of cardboard, which is larger than the top of the bucket, with foil. Put the bucket on the cardboard.
Knot the end of the string, or raffia, and pin it into the cardboard at the bottom.
Take the string up and across the top. Pin it to the board on the opposite side.

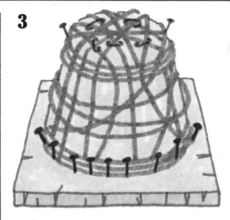

3. Next take the string about 5cm along the side of the base and pin it to the board. Wind it over the top again and down the other side. Where it crosses the other string pin it with a safety pin.
Keep on winding and pinning the string until the bucket is covered.
Put on the apron at this stage and spread newspaper under the project.

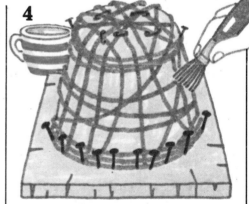

4. Mix a cupful of PVA glue with two cups of water. Brush the mixture over the mask, soaking the string well.
Leave to dry overnight.
When the mask is dry, remove the pins. Re-coat with glue mixture and leave to dry again.

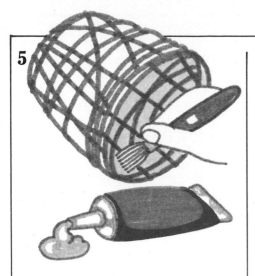

5

Remove the string shape from the bucket and pull away the foil.
5. Paint the inside of the mask with rubber-based glue to make it smooth. Check that all the pins have been taken out.

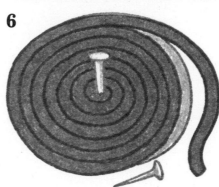

6

To make round eyes

Cut a circle of cardboard the size you want for the eye and cover with foil.
6. Pin the end of a piece of string to the centre and coil it round and round. Pin the end and cut off. Paint with two coats of PVA glue mixture as you did for the mask. Leave to dry and make another eye. Take coil off the cardboard.

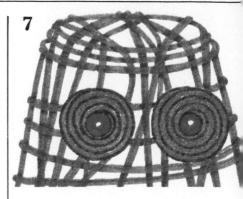

7

7. Finish off the eyes by sticking beads or buttons to the centres to form the pupils.
Decide where to put the eyes. Make sure they do not block your view. Put rubber-based glue on the backs of the eyes and also on the eye positions on the mask.
When the glue is dry it is rubbery enough to hold the eyes if you push them on to the mask.

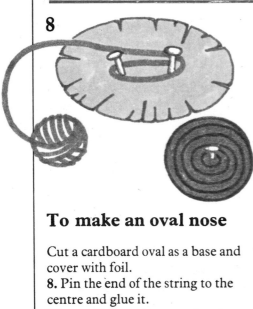

8

To make an oval nose

Cut a cardboard oval as a base and cover with foil.
8. Pin the end of the string to the centre and glue it.
Then coil the string round and paint it with glue as for an eye. Make a smaller circle for the bottom of the nose.

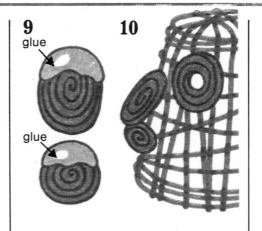

9 10

glue

glue

9. Put glue on the wrong side at the top of the oval and also on the top of the small circle. Put glue on the nose position on the mask.
10. When the glue is dry join the nose sections together with the circle at the bottom and press in place on the mask.

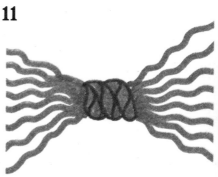

11

To make hair

Cut several pieces of string or raffia each about 40cm long.
11. Tease out the ends of each piece leaving a plain part in the middle. Fold the lengths in half and put glue on the plain parts. When the glue is dry stick them on to the top of the mask.

Mouth and ears

12. Make an oval mouth in the same way as the nose and stick it on. For the ears plait two lengths of string. Stiffen with glue mixture and stick on as for the mouth. Make a loopy topknot with a length of stiffened string or raffia and tie it on.

12

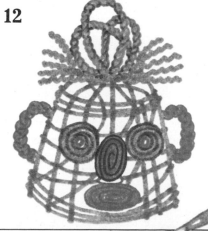

In the photograph

The pointed ears and nose on the centre mask have been shaped on an egg cup. The mask can easily be turned into a bear or a panda. To make a round mask like the one on the right, blow up a balloon, then wind and glue raffia round it. When the PVA glue mixture is dry, pop the balloon with a pin. Then cut a hole in the raffia ball for your head.

Some more trace patterns

Here are some more trace patterns you can use for the glued wool pictures shown on page 10 and for the embroidery stitches on page 12. You'll find the notes on how to do tracings on page 3.